Hair
Styling Tips and Tricks
for Girls

★American Girl®

Thanks to Anastasia, Anna, Christina, Celina, Eileen, Leanna, Mariana, Marisa, and Morgan
for letting us tug on their hair!

Published by American Girl Publishing, Inc.

Questions or comments? Call 1-800-845-0005, visit our Web site at **americangirl.com**,
or write to Customer Service, American Girl, 8400 Fairway Place, Middleton, WI 53562-0497.

Printed in China

08 09 10 11 12 13 14 LEO 28 27 26 25 24 23

Editorial Development: Julie Williams, Michelle Watkins; Grooming Copy: Sarah Jane Brian;
Art Direction: Kym Abrams ; Design: Elaine Leonard, Mengwan Lin, Chris Lorette David;
Production: Kendra Schluter, Janette Sowinski, Jeannette Bailey, Judith Lary, Mindy Rappe;
Illustrations: Shawn Banner; Tabletop Photography: Mike Walker, Jamie Young; Styling: Claire Barbes

Library of Congress Cataloging-in-Publication Data
Hair : styling tips and tricks for girls / hair styling and photography by Jim Jordan.
p. cm. "American girl library."
Summary: Provides advice on taking care of different types of hair, instructions for a variety of hairstyles, and
suggestions for all kinds of hair accessories.
ISBN 978-1-58485-038-0
1. Hairwork—Juvenile literature. 2. Hairstyles—Juvenile literature. 3. Braids (Hairdressing)—Juvenile literature.
4. Hair—Care and hygiene—Juvenile literature. [1. Hair—Care and hygiene.
2. Hairstyles.] I. Jordan, Jim (Jim M.), 1960–ill.
II. American girl (Middleton, Wis.)

TT975 .H35 2000
646.7.24—dc21   00-026642

Dear Reader,

Thick, thin, curly, or straight—no matter what type
of hair you have, good grooming is the key to making
it look and feel great. Get started by taking a quiz to
find your hair type. Then turn the page for grooming
tips tailored to you. Read on to discover the truth
about hair myths, what to do on bad hair days, and
how to get a perfect new cut.

You'll also find step-by-step instructions for lots of
new and classic styles like twists, knots, braids, and
more. Don't miss the special stylist tips for secrets to
keeping your hair looking and feeling great!

Your friends at American Girl

contents

Hair Care & Hair Stuff

Twists & Knots

Terrific Tails

Beautiful Braids

Best Tressed

The Mane Idea

The healthier you are, the healthier your hair will be. Eat a nutritious diet with foods high in protein, such as meats, nuts, and cheeses; whole grains; and fresh fruits and vegetables to help hair grow healthy and strong. Get regular exercise, too—it improves blood circulation and sends nutrients to your scalp, where new hair grows.

Shampoo Clues

Take special care when washing your hair. Rub a quarter-size amount of shampoo into the roots only. Massage your scalp with your fingertips—not your nails. Nails can scratch the skin and damage hair. Scrunch suds through the rest of your hair. Rinse well, and repeat only if your hair is really dirty.

Beat the Heat!

Keep these tips in mind to prevent blow-dryer damage. Blot dripping wet hair with a towel before blow-drying. Hold the dryer at least 6 inches away from your hair. And keep the blow-dryer moving so that you don't aim heat at one part of your head for more than a few seconds at a time.

1. A barrette in your hair usually . . .
   a. won't close unless you try just a tiny bit of hair.
   b. slides right out.
   c. gets hidden because your hair poufs out around it.
   d. clips in with no problem.

2. If you let your hair dry naturally, it takes . . .
   a. forever!
   b. about 30 minutes.
   c. about an hour and a half.
   d. about an hour.

3. If you only brush your hair, it . . .
   a. sticks out in all the wrong places.
   b. lies flat as a pancake on your head.
   c. gets frizzy.
   d. looks fine.

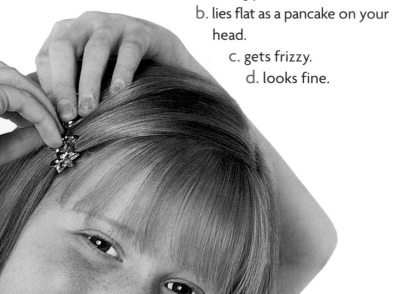

Hair Type?

a.　　　b.　　　c.　　　d.

4. Choose the braid that best matches your hair.

Answer Key
If you picked . . .

All a's: You have thick hair. Turn to page 10 for tips on keeping your hair in top shape.

All b's: You have thin hair. Turn to page 11 for hints to help your hair stay soft and full of body.

All c's: You have curly or coarse hair. Turn to page 12 for ways to keep curls lovely and frizz-free.

All d's: You have medium hair. Your hair is not thick or thin, but right in the middle. Flip to page 13 for hair tips.

A mix of a's, b's, c's, and d's: Your hair is more than one type. For example, you may have hair that is thick and curly, which is very common. Try the tips for different types of hair to see what works for you.

In the Thick . . .

Hair-Care Tips

Use conditioner to keep thick hair soft. But if your scalp gets oily, keep your roots clear of conditioner. Try a gel to get control of full hair and tame frizz.

Styling Tricks

A haircut with long layers can help thin out thick hair.

To straighten out thick waves, blow-dry your hair in sections while pulling straight down with a flat brush. Aim your blow-dryer down, too.

If your hair is straight and thick, you may have a hard time curling it. Spray or rub in a gel before using rollers.

Hair-Care Tips

Wash thin hair often to keep natural scalp oils from weighing hair down. It's best to wash it in the morning, since oils spread at night while you lie on your pillow. Wash with a volumizing shampoo to boost hair's body.

Use conditioner only on the ends of your hair, if necessary. Have healthy hair? Skip the conditioner—it can make hair limp. Banish tangles with a detangler spray or lotion. It's lighter than conditioner.

Styling Tricks

Long locks can weigh hair down and make it flat. Try bangs or layers around your face for a fuller look.

Get an extra boost by blow-drying your hair upside down. Let your hair air-dry partly. Then bend over and blow-dry against the roots. Try styling mousse for more body and hold.

Curls & Whirls

Hair-Care Tips

Curly or coarse hair can be dry because natural oils don't get distributed. Use conditioner every time you shampoo. If your hair is still dry, try a deep-conditioning treatment once or twice a month. A leave-in conditioner helps curls hold their shape.

For very curly or kinky hair, rub a dab of pomade, or hair balm, between your palms and work it through your hair.

Styling Tricks

Keep curls curlier by air-drying when possible. If you do blow-dry, attach a diffuser to your dryer to cut down the flow of air, which prevents frizz.

In the Middle

Hair-Care Tips

If your hair is medium textured and feels healthy, you may not need many styling products. It's a good idea to use conditioner once in a while, but don't use it every day.

Medium hair can be oily at the roots. If so, wash your hair often with an oily hair shampoo. Use conditioner only if the ends are dry.

Be aware of changes in your hair. Hot sun and too much brushing, blow-drying, or hot curling can dry out your hair. Protect your hair by wearing a hat, and use a moisturizing shampoo and conditioner. You can also try a bit of leave-in conditioner on the ends.

Flip Tail

Ponytail Wrap

Flip Tail
Flip for a new twist on the classic ponytail!

1. Hold chin down toward chest and make a low ponytail. Tie off with an elastic.

2. Reach underneath the ponytail and use your finger and thumb to make a hole in the middle of your hair above the elastic.

3. With your other hand, twist the ponytail, grab it with your fingers that are making the hole, and pull it through.

Ponytail Wrap
Use a strand of hair to band a ponytail.

  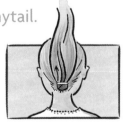

1. Hold chin down toward chest and make a low pony, leaving a 1-inch strand of hair underneath the tail out of the elastic.

2. Wrap the loose strand around the elastic 2 or 3 times.

3. Tuck the rest of the strand into the elastic under the ponytail and pull through. Comb the strand into the tail.

Pigtail Parade

High Pigtails

Gather your hair high on each side of your head and tie off with elastics.

Low Pigtails

Gather hair on each side of your head behind your ears and tie off with elastics.

Looped Pigtails

Make low pigtails, pulling your hair only halfway through the elastics the second time.

Wrapped Pigtails

Make 2 low pigtails, then follow the directions on page 15 for Ponytail Wrap.

'Do-Dads

Hold your hair with pretty pins, cute clips, and fantastic elastics.

Perfect Pins

Bobby pins are great for keeping growing bangs off your face. They can also help keep an updo up and make ponytail strands that stray stay. Be sure the pin's bumpy side is on top—it will hold hair better that way.

Pony Tricks

From fat scrunchies to skinny elastics, there's a perfect ponytail or braid holder for every hair type. Make sure the elastic you pick is covered and snag-free. If your hair is very thin or slick, the elastic may slip out. Give hair more grip by spritzing it with hair spray before you pull it back.

Cute Clips

Jaw clips come in all sizes and open and close like, well, a jaw. Use tiny clips throughout your hair, or use one big clip to hold all of your hair. For the best hold, twist hair a bit before you clip it.

Pool Pigtails

Beach Knot

Pool Pigtails
Beat the heat with a cool hairdo.

1. Make 2 low pig-tails and tie off with elastics.

2. Starting from the top of 1 tail, add more elastics, spacing them evenly. Stylist Tip: Brush tail before adding each elastic.

3. Add elastics to the other pigtail, making sure they are even with the elastics on the first pigtail.

Beach Knot
Slide wet hair into a neat knot.

1. Hold chin down toward chest and make a low pony-tail. Wrap an elastic once around hair. Twist elastic.

2. Pull ponytail halfway through elastic.

3. Let rest of ponytail sprout up or off to the side.

Beautiful Braids

Beautiful Braids

Brush up on your braiding basics.

1. Take a part down the back of your scalp for pigtails.

2. Tie off 1 pigtail. Separate hair from the other pigtail into 3 equal sections.

3. Cross the section on your right over the center section.

4. Cross the section on your left over the center section. Stylist Tip: Keep a tight hold on sections as you cross them.

5. Continue crossing over the center section with right and left sections until hair is braided. Tie off with an elastic and repeat.

Stylist Tip

Before braiding, mist hair with water from a spray bottle to keep your style flyaway-free.

23

Game-Time Tail

All-Star Braids

Game-Time Tail

Make the play in a sporty style.

1. Gather hair from the top and sides of your head and tie off with an elastic at the back of your head.

2. Gather a handful of hair from each side of your head and combine with the first ponytail in back of your head. Tie off.

3. Gather the rest of your hair from each side and combine with hair from first and second ponytails. Tie off with an elastic.

All-Star Braids

With pigtails this neat, you can't be beat!

1. Make low, behind-the-ear pigtails and tie off with elastics. Braid them and tie off again.

2. Wrap an elastic around the top of each braid, twist the elastic, and pull braids halfway through.

3. Tie an elastic halfway down each looped braid to keep hair from coming loose during the game!

Quiz

Hair-Brained Ideas?

1. Cutting hair makes it grow faster.

   True   False

2. Rinsing hair with cold water makes it shinier.

   True   False

3. Hair gets used to the same shampoo after a while, so you should change brands often.

   True   False

4. Brushing your hair one hundred strokes a day will keep it shiny.

   True   False

5. Eating more protein will make your hair thicker.

   True   False

6. Hair grows faster in the summer.

   True   False

Answers

1. False. Trimming can make hair look longer by keeping the ends healthy, so they don't break off or split. Experts recommend a trim at least once every three months.

2. True. Cold water makes the surface of the hair, called the *cuticle*, lie flat. A flat cuticle reflects light better. Blasting hair with cool air after blow-drying gives the same effect. See if your dryer has a cool setting.

3. False. If a shampoo works, keep using it. If conditioners or other products build up and make your hair limp and dull, try a clarifying shampoo. It has special ingredients to get rid of buildup and make your hair extra clean. Most clarifying shampoos shouldn't be used more than once a week, since they can dry hair out.

4. False. Too much brushing roughens and damages hair, which makes it look duller. A few gentle strokes with a natural-bristle brush can add shine, though. Natural brushes spread the oil from your scalp throughout your hair.

5. False. Even though hair is made of protein, burgers won't give you big hair. To make your hair look thicker, try a volumizing shampoo, gel, or mousse. These products coat each strand of hair or make it swell so that it feels thicker.

6. Probably false. Some stylists say hair grows faster when the weather heats up, but there's no scientific evidence for this. On average, hair grows about half an inch per month. So if you're growing out your hair, only one thing can help—patience!

Crowning Twists

Crowning Twists

Roll your hair into rows of twists.

1. Using a comb, separate hair on crown of head into 5 even sections, as shown. Clip sections off with mini clips.

2. Remove clip from center section, separate an inch of hair, and begin twisting it back across the top of your head.

3 Pick up more hair from the section as you move toward the back of your head, rolling hair into the twist.

4. Stop twisting and rolling about halfway toward the back of your head and secure section with a mini clip.

5. Repeat until all 5 sections are twisted.

Nifty Knots

Nifty Knots

Twist your hair into "teddy bear" ears.

1. Make 2 high pigtails and tie off with elastics. Starting on one side, twist pigtail until it begins to coil up on itself.

2. Keep a firm hold on the end of the pigtail and tie it into a knot, pushing the knot down around the elastic.

3. Coil the rest of the twisted pigtail around the knot. Tuck ends underneath knot.

4. Insert bobby pins into knot, crisscrossing them and pinning hair from both your scalp and the knot. Repeat on the other side.

Low Knots

Make Nifty Knots at the nape of your neck. Start with 2 low pigtails, twist, and follow Steps 2–4.

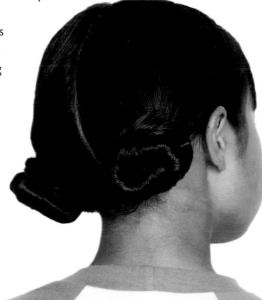

Twist & Shout

Knotted Ponies

Divide hair on the crown of your head into 3 sections. Tie each into a mini ponytail and knot (see Step 2 of Nifty Knots on page 31).

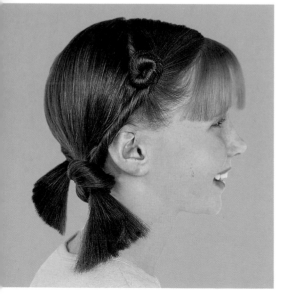

Knotted Pigtails

Twist and coil a section of hair from the front of your head. Pin coil on side of head. Pull leftover twisted hair back into a low pigtail with the rest of hair on one side of your head. Tie off with an elastic, then knot.

Bunny Twist

Make Crowning Twists (see page 28) on the top of your head. Then twist with your loose hair into a bun (see Ballet Bun on page 36).

Clippy Twists

Twist and knot sections of hair from your crown. Then gather with the rest of your hair into a ponytail. Sprinkle with clips.

Hair Thingies

Barrette Beauties

Barrettes can add sparkle to almost any 'do. But choose carefully. Barrettes made to hold a lot of hair can slip out of thin hair. Check the clasp before you buy to make sure it works well. For delicate hair, avoid barrettes with sharp metal clasps. They can break or damage hair.

Get Creative

Spice up your style with out-of-the-ordinary accessories. Wind your wisps into corkscrews. Sprinkle your strands with hair snaps. You can even "do up your 'do" with things around the house, like shoelaces or ribbons!

Band Practice

Headbands are great for a quick and pretty hair fix. They can be thin or thick, made of elastic, plastic, or metal. Some have teeth to grip hair better. Pick one that feels comfortable. If it's too tight, you may get a headache. If it's too loose, it will fall right out.

35

Ballet Bun

Ballet Bun

Twirl your hair into an elegant bun.

1. Gather hair at the back of your head and make a high ponytail. Tie off with an elastic.

2. Twist ponytail tightly. Stylist Tip: Spritz ponytail with hair spray to keep any shorter ends from popping out.

3. Wrap twisted ponytail around the elastic.

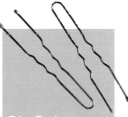

4. Tuck the end of the ponytail under the coil, or *bun*, and insert a bobby pin to hold.

5. Pin the rest of the bun in place, crisscrossing bobby pins or hairpins and grabbing hair from both your scalp and the bun.

Pin Pointers

U-shaped hairpins are perfect for pinning thick hair into a bun. Bobby pins, which are closed up, are best for holding medium to thin hair.

Hair Helpers

3 Tangle Tamers

- Stop tangles before they start! Braid long hair or put it in a ponytail before swimming or going out on a windy day.
- Give hair a quick brush before you shower. Pat—don't rub—freshly washed tresses with a towel.
- Use a wide-tooth comb to get rid of tangles. Start at the ends of your hair and work your way up. If a tangle just won't budge, try rubbing conditioner on the knot.

2 Static Busters

- Spritz hair spray onto a brush and run it through your hair.
- Mist hair with a spray-on, leave-in conditioner.

1 Split-End Saver

- Sorry, but there's really only one solution for split ends: snip 'em! To prevent future splits, use conditioner on the ends of your hair to keep them from drying out.

Windup Braids

Top Knot

Windup Braids

Coil pigtail braids into twisty knots.

1. Make 2 high pigtails and tie off with elastics. Braid the pigtails and tie off.

2. Knot each braid around the top elastic.

3. Coil the rest of the braid around each knot. Insert bobby pins to hold in place.

Top Knot

Turn a high ponytail into a sprouty knot.

1. Brush hair on top of head and tie off with an elastic.

2. Twist ponytail and tie into a knot around the elastic. Stylist Tip: Unwashed hair works best. Natural oils make hair easier to hold.

3. Insert bobby pins, pinning hair near scalp and in knot. Finger-comb sprout at top.

41

Rope Braid

Rope Braid

Twist your ponytail into a rope.

1. Holding chin down toward chest, brush hair back into a low ponytail. Tie off with an elastic.

2. Separate the ponytail into 2 equal sections.

3. Tightly cross 1 section over the other until you reach the end of the ponytail.

4. Tie off with another elastic.

Stylist Tip

The Rope Braid works best on really long hair. If your rope braid unrolls, try again, this time wetting your hair before "braiding."

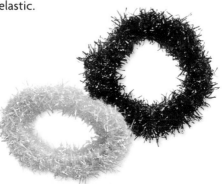

French Braids

Practice makes perfect with this classic style!

1. Make a part down the back of your head for pigtails. Use an elastic to hold 1 section off to the side.

2. On the other side, gather hair from the front of your head and separate it into 3 even sections.

3. Begin by crossing over the sections once, as you would for a regular braid.

4. Grab a few strands of hair to the left of the braid and add it to the left-hand section. Cross the section over the center.

5. Grab a few strands of hair to the right of the braid and add it to the right-hand section. Cross the section over the center.

6. Repeat until all hair has been added; then continue with a regular braid. Tie off with an elastic. Repeat on the other side.

Braid Craze

Framing Braids

Make a side part and French-braid a section of hair across your crown and down the side. Make a regular braid on the other side of your face.

Bunny Braids

Begin with a crooked part and braid small sections of hair. Gather braids with loose hair and twist into a bun (see Ballet Bun on page 37).

Mini Braids

Braid small sections of
hair all over your head.
Tie them off with color-
ful elastics.

Ribbon Braids

Knot the center of a
ribbon around a small
section of hair. Separate
hair into 2 smaller sec-
tions and braid, using
the ribbon as the third
section.

Pony Detail

Lace It Up

Wrap your ponytail with silk cord, ribbon, or even leather shoelaces. Make a low ponytail and tie off with an elastic at the top and the bottom. Knot the center of a leather shoelace around the top elastic. Wrap the 2 ends of the shoelace down the length of the ponytail, crisscrossing every inch or so. Tie off at the end in a small bow.

Twinkle Tail

Add sparkle to your pony with mini clips. Just make a low ponytail, fluff up the tail, and sprinkle with twinkling jewels.

All in a Row

Decorate your ponytail with bejeweled ponytail ties or barrettes. Make a low ponytail at the nape of your neck and add baubles down the length of your hair for a simple, pretty tail.

Ponytail Veil

Ponytail Veil

Weave your hair into a pretty ponytail veil.

1. Make 3 mini ponytails on the crown of your head: 1 in the middle, 1 on the right, and 1 on the left. Tie off with elastics.

2. Separate the middle ponytail into 2 sections.

3. Combine the right-hand section with the ponytail on the right and tie off with an elastic.

4. Combine the left-hand section with the ponytail on the left and tie off with an elastic.

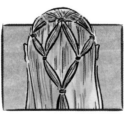

5. Bring the 2 new ponytails to the center and make 1 big ponytail. Tie off with an elastic.

Add More Layers

Try starting this style with 5 mini ponies. You'll have another layer when you're finished!

Make Waves!

Dreamy Waves

Before you braid, think about how big you want your kinks and waves to be and how high you want them to start on your head. The smaller the braid, the more waves you'll get. The higher you start braiding, the more volume you'll get on top.

Bedtime Braids

Before bed, wet your hair thoroughly in the shower or with a spray bottle. Comb out excess water and make braids all over your head. Braid down as close to the ends of your hair as possible to prevent frizzies. Sweet dreams!

Rise and Shine

When you wake up, your braids will be dry. Remove the elastics and carefully finger-comb hair apart. Don't use a brush! To tame any unwanted frizz, scrunch a little gel through your waves.

Sleep the braided way to kinks and curls.

Curly Cues

Rules of the Roll

- Spray hair lightly with gel before you curl to help hold ringlets and waves.

- For loose, wavy curls, use large rollers. For tight curls, use small rollers.

- Wrap the roller in the direction you want your hair to go. For example, if you wind your hair away from your face, that's how the curl will fall.

- Start at the top of your head and work down.

- Don't brush curls! Shake them into place with your fingertips or use a wide-tooth comb or pick. But if curls are too tight, gently use a brush to loosen the wave.

Twisty Tools

Self-sticking rollers add body and volume.

Hot rollers use heat to lock in curls. Just don't remove them until they've cooled!

Sponge spools are great for making spiral curls.

Bendable stick rollers let you be creative.

Basic Roll

Plan out your 'do and then follow these steps.

1. Take a section of hair about as wide as your roller. Brush it out away from your head. Use less hair for small rollers, more for big ones.

2. Grab a roller, place it at the end of the section of hair, and start rolling. Make sure the ends of your hair are not bent or folded over.

3. When the roller reaches your scalp, clip or secure it in place. Repeat.

Holiday Twist

Sweep hair off shoulders for special occasions.

1. Gather hair at the back of your head, as if you were making a low ponytail.

2. Twist hair to the end while slowly pulling up, making a roll. Stylist Tip: Spray with hair spray to tame stray hairs.

3. Coil remaining twisted hair at the top of the roll.

4. Insert bobby pins around the coil and the roll to hold in place. Be sure to pin hair in the coil and roll as well as near your scalp.

Barrette Twist

Follow Steps 1 and 2. Hold hair up with one hand and insert a barrette through the middle of the roll. Clip to hair near scalp.

Braidy Bunch

Tiny Tails

Braidy Bunch

Get loopy with your braids for slumber-party fun.

1. Make 2 pigtails and tie off with elastics. Divide 1 pigtail into 3 sections.

2. Divide each section into 3 smaller sections and braid. Tie off with elastics.

3. Tie another, larger elastic at the top of braids and loop ends through the elastic at the top of the braid. Repeat on the other side.

Tiny Tails

Wake up your hair with perky mini ponies.

1. Using a tail comb, separate a tiny section from rest of hair. Tie off with a small elastic.

2. Continue making as many mini ponies as you'd like. Tie off with brightly colored elastics.

Stylist Tip

Want to add some lift to your hair? Make Tiny Tails all over your head. After a few hours, remove elastics and pouf!

Haircut Corner

Getting a new 'do? Follow these steps for salon success to get the cut you crave!

1. Bring a picture of the style to the salon. Clip a few choices from magazines. Can't find a picture? Be sure to clearly explain the look you want.

2. Be realistic. If your hair is thin and short, a haircut won't make it long and full. Ask the stylist if the cut you want will work with your hair type.

3. Tell your stylist how much time you have for your hair. If you're always running from swimming practice to violin lessons, you don't want a cut that needs 25 minutes of blow-drying.

4. Don't be shy! Tell the person washing your hair if the water is too hot or too cold.

5. Sit straight up in the stylist's chair and hold still. Keep an eye on things in the mirror.

6. Speak up if you don't like your cut. The stylist may be able to make some last-minute changes.

7. Before you leave, don't forget to ask for styling tips.

8. Enjoy your new look. But remember, healthy hair that makes you happy is the best look of all!

Write to us!

Hair **Editor**
American Girl
8400 Fairway Place
Middleton, WI 53562

All comments and suggestions received by American Girl
may be used without compensation or acknowledgment.
Sorry—photos can't be returned.

Here are some other American Girl books you might like:

❏ I read it.

❏ I read it.

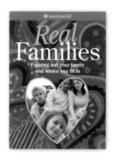

❏ I read it.

❏ I read it.

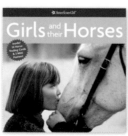

❏ I read it.

❏ I read it.